MznLnx

Missing Links Exam Preps

Exam Prep for

Product Management

Lehmann & Winer, 4th Edition

The MznLnx Exam Prep is your link from the texbook and lecture to your exams.
The MznLnx Exam Preps are unauthorized and comprehensive reviews of your textbooks.

All material provided by MznLnx and Rico Publications (c) 2010
Textbook publishers and textbook authors do not particpate in or contribute to these reviews.

MznLnx

Rico
Publications

Exam Prep for Product Management
4th Edition
Lehmann & Winer

Publisher: Raymond Houge
Assistant Editor: Michael Rouger
Text and Cover Designer: Lisa Buckner
Marketing Manager: Sara Swagger
Project Manager, Editorial Production: Jerry Emerson
Art Director: Vernon Lowerui

Product Manager: Dave Mason
Editorial Assitant: Rachel Guzmanji
Pedagogy: Debra Long
Cover Image: Jim Reed/Getty Images
Text and Cover Printer: City Printing, Inc.
Compositor: Media Mix, Inc.

(c) 2010 Rico Publications
ALL RIGHTS RESERVED. No part of this work
covered by the copyright may be reproduced or
used in any form or by an means--graphic, electronic,
or mechanical, including photocopying, recording,
taping, Web distribution, information storage, and
retrieval systems, or in any other manner--without the
written permission of the publisher.

Printed in the United States
ISBN:

For more information about our products, contact us at:
Dave.Mason@RicoPublications.com

For permission to use material from this text or
product, submit a request online to:
Dave.Mason@RicoPublications.com

Contents

CHAPTER 1
Introduction to Product Management — 1

CHAPTER 2
Marketing Planning — 3

CHAPTER 3
Defining the Competitive Set — 6

CHAPTER 4
Category Attractiveness Analysis — 8

CHAPTER 5
Competitor Analysis — 12

CHAPTER 6
Customer Analysis — 20

CHAPTER 7
Market Potential and Sales Forecasting — 23

CHAPTER 8
Developing Product Strategy — 27

CHAPTER 9
New Products — 31

CHAPTER 10
Pricing Decisions — 33

CHAPTER 11
Advertising Decisions — 38

CHAPTER 12
Promotions — 42

CHAPTER 13
Channel Management — 45

CHAPTER 14
Customer Relationship Management — 49

CHAPTER 15
Financial Analysis for Product Management — 53

CHAPTER 16
Marketing Metrics — 58

ANSWER KEY — 60

TO THE STUDENT

COMPREHENSIVE

The *MznLnx* Exam Prep series is designed to help you pass your exams. Editors at MznLnx review your textbooks and then prepare these practice exams to help you master the textbook material. Unlike study guides, workbooks, and practice tests provided by the texbook publisher and textbook authors, *MznLnx* gives you **all** of the material in each chapter in exam form, not just samples, so you can be sure to nail your exam.

MECHANICAL

The MznLnx Exam Prep series creates exams that will help you learn the subject matter as well as test you on your understanding. Each question is designed to help you master the concept. Just working through the exams, you gain an understanding of the subject--its a simple mechanical process that produces success.

INTEGRATED STUDY GUIDE AND REVIEW

MznLnx is not just a set of exams designed to test you, its also a comprehensive review of the subject content. Each exam question is also a review of the concept, making sure that you will get the answer correct without having to go to other sources of material. You learn as you go! Its the easiest way to pass an exam.

HUMOR

Studying can be tedious and dry. MznLnx's instructional design includes moderate humor within the exam questions on occassion, to break the tedium and revitalize the brain

Chapter 1. Introduction to Product Management

1. A _____ researches, selects, develops, and places a company's products.

   A _____ considers numerous factors such as target demographic, the products offered by the competition, and how well the product fits in with the company's business model. Generally, a _____ manages one or more tangible products.

   a. Product manager
   b. 1990 Clean Air Act
   c. 33 Strategies of War
   d. 28-hour day

2. _____ is an integrated communications-based process through which individuals and communities discover that existing and newly-identified needs and wants may be satisfied by the products and services of others.

   _____ is defined by the American _____ Association as the activity, set of institutions, and processes for creating, communicating, delivering, and exchanging offerings that have value for customers, clients, partners, and society at large. The term developed from the original meaning which referred literally to going to market, as in shopping, or going to a market to buy or sell goods or services.

   a. Market development
   b. Disruptive technology
   c. Marketing
   d. Customer relationship management

3. Procter is a surname, and may also refer to:

   - Bryan Waller Procter (pseud. Barry Cornwall), English poet
   - Goodwin Procter, American law firm
   - _____, consumer products multinational

   a. Master and Servant Acts
   b. Procter ' Gamble
   c. Downstream
   d. Strict liability

4. A _____ is a written document that details the necessary actions to achieve one or more marketing objectives. It can be for a product or service, a brand, or a product line. _____s cover between one and five years.

a. Marketing plan
b. Market development
c. Disruptive technology
d. Marketing strategy

5. _____ is a broad label that refers to any individuals or households that use goods and services generated within the economy. The concept of a _____ is used in different contexts, so that the usage and significance of the term may vary.

Typically when business people and economists talk of _____s they are talking about person as _____, an aggregated commodity item with little individuality other than that expressed in the buy/not-buy decision.

a. 33 Strategies of War
b. 1990 Clean Air Act
c. 28-hour day
d. Consumer

Chapter 2. Marketing Planning

1. _____ is an integrated communications-based process through which individuals and communities discover that existing and newly-identified needs and wants may be satisfied by the products and services of others.

   _____ is defined by the American _____ Association as the activity, set of institutions, and processes for creating, communicating, delivering, and exchanging offerings that have value for customers, clients, partners, and society at large. The term developed from the original meaning which referred literally to going to market, as in shopping, or going to a market to buy or sell goods or services.

   a. Disruptive technology
   b. Customer relationship management
   c. Market development
   d. Marketing

2. A _____ is a written document that details the necessary actions to achieve one or more marketing objectives. It can be for a product or service, a brand, or a product line. _____s cover between one and five years.
   a. Marketing plan
   b. Market development
   c. Disruptive technology
   d. Marketing strategy

3. _____ is an organization's process of defining its strategy and making decisions on allocating its resources to pursue this strategy, including its capital and people. Various business analysis techniques can be used in _____, including SWOT analysis (Strengths, Weaknesses, Opportunities, and Threats) and PEST analysis (Political, Economic, Social, and Technological analysis) or STEER analysis involving Socio-cultural, Technological, Economic, Ecological, and Regulatory factors and EPISTEL (Environment, Political, Informatic, Social, Technological, Economic and Legal)

   _____ is the formal consideration of an organization's future course. All _____ deals with at least one of three key questions:

   1. 'What do we do?'
   2. 'For whom do we do it?'
   3. 'How do we excel?'

In business _____, the third question is better phrased 'How can we beat or avoid competition?'. (Bradford and Duncan, page 1.)

   a. Strategic Planning
   b. 1990 Clean Air Act
   c. 33 Strategies of War
   d. 28-hour day

4. _____ is a worldwide management consulting firm that focuses on solving issues of concern to senior management. McKinsey serves as an advisor to the world's leading businesses, governments, and institutions. It is widely recognized as a leader and one of the most prestigious firms in the management consulting industry.

   a. 28-hour day
   b. 33 Strategies of War
   c. McKinsey ' Company
   d. 1990 Clean Air Act

5. Procter is a surname, and may also refer to:

   - Bryan Waller Procter (pseud. Barry Cornwall), English poet
   - Goodwin Procter, American law firm
   - _____, consumer products multinational

   a. Master and Servant Acts
   b. Strict liability
   c. Downstream
   d. Procter ' Gamble

6. A _____ is a process that can allow an organization to concentrate its limited resources on the greatest opportunities to increase sales and achieve a sustainable competitive advantage. A _____ should be centered around the key concept that customer satisfaction is the main goal.

   A _____ is a written plan which combines product development, promotion, distribution, and pricing approach, identifies the firm's marketing goals, and explains how they will be achieved within a stated timeframe.

   a. Product bundling
   b. Disruptive technology
   c. Category management
   d. Marketing strategy

7. _____ is a business magazine published by McGraw-Hill. It was first published in 1929 (as The Business Week) under the direction of Malcolm Muir, who was serving as president of the McGraw-Hill Publishing company at the time. Its primary competitors in the national business magazine category are Fortune and Forbes, which are published bi-weekly.

a. Democracy in America
b. The Wealth of Nations
c. Hotel Vikas
d. BusinessWeek

6   Chapter 3. Defining the Competitive Set

1. _____ SE or _____ is a German manufacturer of luxury automobiles, which is majority-owned by the _____ and Pi>ĕch families. _____ SE holds two chief assets, the first of which is Dr. Ing. h.c. F.
   a. Porsche
   b. Michael David Capellas
   c. Adam Smith
   d. Abraham Harold Maslow

2. _____ is an advertisement in which a particular product specifically mentions a competitor by name for the express purpose of showing why the competitor is inferior to the product naming it.

This should not be confused with parody advertisements, where a fictional product is being advertised for the purpose of poking fun at the particular advertisement, nor should it be confused with the use of a coined brand name for the purpose of comparing the product without actually naming an actual competitor. ('Wikipedia tastes better and is less filling than the Encyclopedia Galactica.')

In the 1980s, during what has been referred to as the cola wars, soft-drink manufacturer Pepsi ran a series of advertisements where people, caught on hidden camera, in a blind taste test, chose Pepsi over rival Coca-Cola.

   a. 28-hour day
   b. 1990 Clean Air Act
   c. 33 Strategies of War
   d. Comparative advertising

3. Procter is a surname, and may also refer to:

   - Bryan Waller Procter (pseud. Barry Cornwall), English poet
   - Goodwin Procter, American law firm
   - _____, consumer products multinational

   a. Master and Servant Acts
   b. Procter ' Gamble
   c. Strict liability
   d. Downstream

4. _____ is a graphics technique used by asset marketers that attempts to visually display the perceptions of customers or potential customers. Typically the position of a product, product line, brand, or company is displayed relative to their competition.

Perceptual maps can have any number of dimensions but the most common is two dimensions.

a. PEST analysis
b. Product differentiation
c. Mass marketing
d. Perceptual mapping

Chapter 4. Category Attractiveness Analysis

1. Procter is a surname, and may also refer to:

   - Bryan Waller Procter (pseud. Barry Cornwall), English poet
   - Goodwin Procter, American law firm
   - _____, consumer products multinational

   a. Strict liability
   b. Downstream
   c. Master and Servant Acts
   d. Procter ' Gamble

2. _____ Management is the succession of strategies used by management as a product goes through its _____. The conditions in which a product is sold changes over time and must be managed as it moves through its succession of stages.

   The _____ goes through many phases, involves many professional disciplines, and requires many skills, tools and processes.

   a. Strategic Alliance
   b. Golden handshake
   c. Job hunting
   d. Product life cycle

3. In statistics, many time series exhibit cyclic variation known as _____, periodic variation, or periodic fluctuations. This variation can be either regular or semiregular.

   For example, retail sales tend to peak for the Christmas season and then decline after the holidays.

   a. 1990 Clean Air Act
   b. 33 Strategies of War
   c. 28-hour day
   d. Seasonality

4. The _____ is a bank regulation, which sets a framework on how banks and depository institutions must handle their capital. The categorization of assets and capital is highly standardized so that it can be risk weighted. Internationally, the Basel Committee on Banking Supervision housed at the Bank for International Settlements influence each country's banking _____s.

Chapter 4. Category Attractiveness Analysis

   a. Capital requirement
   b. Reserve requirement
   c. 1990 Clean Air Act
   d. Lock box

5. _____, in microeconomics, are the cost advantages that a business obtains due to expansion. They are factors that cause a producer's average cost per unit to fall as scale is increased. _____ is a long run concept and refers to reductions in unit cost as the size of a facility, or scale, increases.
   a. Economies of scope
   b. A Stake in the Outcome
   c. A4e
   d. Economies of scale

6. In marketing, _____ is the process of distinguishing the differences of a product or offering from others, to make it more attractive to a particular target market. This involves differentiating it from competitors' products as well as one's own product offerings.
   a. Market share
   b. PEST analysis
   c. Market development
   d. Product differentiation

7. _____ is one of the four elements of marketing mix. An organization or set of organizations (go-betweens) involved in the process of making a product or service available for use or consumption by a consumer or business user.

The other three parts of the marketing mix are product, pricing, and promotion.

   a. Distribution
   b. Job creation programs
   c. Matching theory
   d. Missing completely at random

8. Switching barriers or _____s are terms used in microeconomics, strategic management, and marketing to describe any impediment to a customer's changing of suppliers.

In many markets, consumers are forced to incur costs when switching from one supplier to another. These costs are called _____s and can come in many different shapes.

a. Strategic group
b. Strategic business unit
c. Switching cost
d. Corporate strategy

9. In economics, business, retail, and accounting, a _____ is the value of money that has been used up to produce something, and hence is not available for use anymore. In economics, a _____ is an alternative that is given up as a result of a decision. In business, the _____ may be one of acquisition, in which case the amount of money expended to acquire it is counted as _____.

a. Cost overrun
b. Cost
c. Cost allocation
d. Fixed costs

10. _____ is a broad label that refers to any individuals or households that use goods and services generated within the economy. The concept of a _____ is used in different contexts, so that the usage and significance of the term may vary.

Typically when business people and economists talk of _____s they are talking about person as _____, an aggregated commodity item with little individuality other than that expressed in the buy/not-buy decision.

a. 28-hour day
b. 1990 Clean Air Act
c. 33 Strategies of War
d. Consumer

11. _____ is a concept related to the relative abilities of parties in a situation to exert influence over each other. If both parties are on an equal footing in a debate, then they will have equal _____, such as in a perfectly competitive market, or between an evenly matched monopoly and monopsony.

There are a number of fields where the concept of _____ has proven crucial to coherent analysis: game theory, labour economics, collective bargaining arrangements, diplomatic negotiations, settlement of litigation, the price of insurance, and any negotiation in general.

a. Buy-sell agreement
b. Bargaining power
c. 1990 Clean Air Act
d. Trade credit

12. In finance, the _____s between two currencies specifies how much one currency is worth in terms of the other. It is the value of a foreign nation's currency in terms of the home nation's currency. For example an _____ of 102 Japanese yen to the United States dollar means that JPY 102 is worth the same as USD 1.
  a. A4e
  b. AAAI
  c. Exchange rate
  d. A Stake in the Outcome

Chapter 5. Competitor Analysis

1. Procter is a surname, and may also refer to:

   - Bryan Waller Procter (pseud. Barry Cornwall), English poet
   - Goodwin Procter, American law firm
   - _____, consumer products multinational

   a. Strict liability
   b. Master and Servant Acts
   c. Downstream
   d. Procter ' Gamble

2. An _____ is a comprehensive report on a company's activities throughout the preceding year. _____s are intended to give shareholders and other interested persons information about the company's activities and financial performance. Most jurisdictions require companies to prepare and disclose _____s, and many require the _____ to be filed at the company's registry.

   a. AAAI
   b. A4e
   c. A Stake in the Outcome
   d. Annual report

3. _____ is a business magazine published by McGraw-Hill. It was first published in 1929 (as The Business Week) under the direction of Malcolm Muir, who was serving as president of the McGraw-Hill Publishing company at the time. Its primary competitors in the national business magazine category are Fortune and Forbes, which are published bi-weekly.

   a. The Wealth of Nations
   b. BusinessWeek
   c. Hotel Vikas
   d. Democracy in America

4. A _____ is a set of exclusive rights granted by a state to an inventor or his assignee for a limited period of time in exchange for a disclosure of an invention.

   The procedure for granting _____s, the requirements placed on the _____ee and the extent of the exclusive rights vary widely between countries according to national laws and international agreements. Typically, however, a _____ application must include one or more claims defining the invention which must be new, inventive, and useful or industrially applicable.

a. Labor Management Reporting and Disclosure Act
b. Federal Trade Commission Act
c. Food, Drug, and Cosmetic Act
d. Patent

5. A _____ is a distinctive sign or indicator used by an individual, business organization, or other legal entity to identify that the products and/or services to consumers with which the _____ appears originate from a unique source and to distinguish its products or services from those of other entities.
   a. Virtual team
   b. Succession planning
   c. Kanban
   d. Trademark

6. A _____ is a professional who provides advice in a particular area of expertise such as management, accountancy, the environment, entertainment, technology, law , human resources, marketing, medicine, finance, economics, public affairs, communication, engineering, sound system design, graphic design, or waste management.

A _____ is usually an expert or a professional in a specific field and has a wide knowledge of the subject matter. A _____ usually works for a consultancy firm or is self-employed, and engages with multiple and changing clients.

   a. 1990 Clean Air Act
   b. 33 Strategies of War
   c. Consultant
   d. 28-hour day

7. An _____ is an organization founded and funded by businesses that operate in a specific industry. An industry trade association participates in public relations activities such as advertising, education, political donations, lobbying and publishing, but its main focus is collaboration between companies, or standardization. Associations may offer other services, such as producing conferences, networking or charitable events or offering classes or educational materials.
   a. Industry trade group
   b. A Stake in the Outcome
   c. AAAI
   d. A4e

Chapter 5. Competitor Analysis

8. The _____ is an agency of the United States Department of Health and Human Services and is responsible for regulating and supervising the safety of foods, dietary supplements, drugs, vaccines, biological medical products, blood products, medical devices, radiation-emitting devices, veterinary products, and cosmetics. The FDA also enforces section 361 of the Public Health Service Act and the associated regulations, including sanitation requirements on interstate travel as well as specific rules for control of disease on products ranging from pet turtles to semen donations for assisted reproductive medicine techniques.

The FDA is an agency within the United States Department of Health and Human Services responsible for protecting and promoting the nation's public health.

  a. 28-hour day
  b. 1990 Clean Air Act
  c. Food and Drug Administration
  d. 33 Strategies of War

9. _____ is an advertisement in which a particular product specifically mentions a competitor by name for the express purpose of showing why the competitor is inferior to the product naming it.

This should not be confused with parody advertisements, where a fictional product is being advertised for the purpose of poking fun at the particular advertisement, nor should it be confused with the use of a coined brand name for the purpose of comparing the product without actually naming an actual competitor. ('Wikipedia tastes better and is less filling than the Encyclopedia Galactica.')

In the 1980s, during what has been referred to as the cola wars, soft-drink manufacturer Pepsi ran a series of advertisements where people, caught on hidden camera, in a blind taste test, chose Pepsi over rival Coca-Cola.

  a. 28-hour day
  b. 33 Strategies of War
  c. 1990 Clean Air Act
  d. Comparative advertising

10. A _____ is a process in which a potential employee is evaluated by an employer for prospective employment in their company, organization and was established in the late 16th century.

A _____ typically precedes the hiring decision, and is used to evaluate the candidate. The interview is usually preceded by the evaluation of submitted résumés from interested candidates, then selecting a small number of candidates for interviews.

a. Split shift
b. Payrolling
c. Supported employment
d. Job interview

11. _____ is the process of comparing the cost, cycle time, productivity, or quality of a specific process or method to another that is widely considered to be an industry standard or best practice. Essentially, _____ provides a snapshot of the performance of your business and helps you understand where you are in relation to a particular standard. The result is often a business case for making changes in order to make improvements.
a. Benchmarking
b. Cost leadership
c. Complementors
d. Competitive heterogeneity

12. _____ is the process of discovering the technological principles of a device, object or system through analysis of its structure, function and operation. It often involves taking something (e.g., a mechanical device, electronic component, or software program) apart and analyzing its workings in detail to be used in maintenance, or to try to make a new device or program that does the same thing without copying anything from the original.

_____ has its origins in the analysis of hardware for commercial or military advantage .

a. 28-hour day
b. 1990 Clean Air Act
c. Predictive maintenance
d. Reverse engineering

13. _____ is a form of communication that typically attempts to persuade potential customers to purchase or to consume more of a particular brand of product or service. 'While now central to the contemporary global economy and the reproduction of global production networks, it is only quite recently that _____ has been more than a marginal influence on patterns of sales and production. The formation of modern _____ was intimately bound up with the emergence of new forms of monopoly capitalism around the end of the 19th and beginning of the 20th century as one element in corporate strategies to create, organize and where possible control markets, especially for mass produced consumer goods.
a. A4e
b. AAAI
c. A Stake in the Outcome
d. Advertising

Chapter 5. Competitor Analysis

14. A _____, in the field of business and marketing, is a geographic region or demographic group used to gauge the viability of a product or service in the mass market prior to a wide scale roll-out. The criteria used to judge the acceptability of a _____ region or group include:

1. a population that is demographically similar to the proposed target market; and
2. relative isolation from densely populated media markets so that advertising to the test audience can be efficient and economical.

The _____ ideally aims to duplicate 'everything' - promotion and distribution as well as `product' - on a smaller scale. The technique replicates, typically in one area, what is planned to occur in a national launch; and the results are very carefully monitored, so that they can be extrapolated to projected national results. The `area' may be any one of the following:

- Television area

internet online test

- Test town
- Residential neighborhood
- Test site

A number of decisions have to be taken about any _____:

- Which _____?
- What is to be tested?
- How long a test?
- What are the success criteria?

The simple go or no-go decision, together with the related reduction of risk, is normally the main justification for the expense of _____s. At the same time, however, such _____s can be used to test specific elements of a new product's marketing mix; possibly the version of the product itself, the promotional message and media spend, the distribution channels and the price.

a. 1990 Clean Air Act
b. 28-hour day
c. 33 Strategies of War
d. Test market

15. A broad definition of _____ is the action of gathering, analyzing, and distributing information about products, customers, competitors and any aspect of the environment needed to support executives and managers in making strategic decisions for an organization.

Chapter 5. Competitor Analysis

Key points of this definitions:

1. _____ is an ethical and legal business practice. (This is important as _____ professionals emphasize that the discipline is not the same as industrial espionage which is both unethical and usually illegal.)
2. The focus is on the external business environment.
3. There is a process involved in gathering information, converting it into intelligence and then utilizing this in business decision making. _____ professionals emphasize that if the intelligence gathered is not usable (or actionable) then it is not intelligence.

A more focused definition of _____ regards it as the organizational function responsible for the early identification of risks and opportunities in the market before they become obvious. Experts also call this process the early signal analysis. This definition focuses attention on the difference between dissemination of widely available factual information (such as market statistics, financial reports, newspaper clippings) performed by functions such as libraries and information centers, and _____ which is a perspective on developments and events aimed at yielding a competitive edge.

a. Competitive Intelligence
b. 1990 Clean Air Act
c. 28-hour day
d. Competitor or Competitive Intelligence

16. In marketing, _____ has come to mean the process by which marketers try to create an image or identity in the minds of their target market for its product, brand, or organization. It is the 'relative competitive comparison' their product occupies in a given market as perceived by the target market.

Re-_____ involves changing the identity of a product, relative to the identity of competing products, in the collective minds of the target market.

a. Customer analytics
b. PEST analysis
c. Context analysis
d. Positioning

17. _____ is an integrated communications-based process through which individuals and communities discover that existing and newly-identified needs and wants may be satisfied by the products and services of others.

_____ is defined by the American _____ Association as the activity, set of institutions, and processes for creating, communicating, delivering, and exchanging offerings that have value for customers, clients, partners, and society at large. The term developed from the original meaning which referred literally to going to market, as in shopping, or going to a market to buy or sell goods or services.

  a. Disruptive technology
  b. Customer relationship management
  c. Market development
  d. Marketing

18. A _____ is a process that can allow an organization to concentrate its limited resources on the greatest opportunities to increase sales and achieve a sustainable competitive advantage. A _____ should be centered around the key concept that customer satisfaction is the main goal.

A _____ is a written plan which combines product development, promotion, distribution, and pricing approach, identifies the firm's marketing goals, and explains how they will be achieved within a stated timeframe.

  a. Category management
  b. Disruptive technology
  c. Product bundling
  d. Marketing strategy

19. The _____ is a concept from business management that was first described and popularized by Michael Porter in his 1985 best-seller, Competitive Advantage: Creating and Sustaining Superior Performance.

A _____ is a chain of activities. Products pass through all activities of the chain in order and at each activity the product gains some value. The chain of activities gives the products more added value than the sum of added values of all activities. It is important not to mix the concept of the _____ with the costs occurring throughout the activities.

  a. Mass marketing
  b. Customer relationship management
  c. Market development
  d. Value chain

Chapter 5. Competitor Analysis

20. The _____ is generally accepted as the use and specification of the 'four P's' describing the strategic position of a product in the marketplace. One version of the _____ originated in 1948 when James Culliton said that a marketing decision should be a result of something similar to a recipe. This version was used in 1953 when Neil Borden, in his American Marketing Association presidential address, took the recipe idea one step further and coined the term 'marketing-mix'.
    a. Marketing mix
    b. 1990 Clean Air Act
    c. 33 Strategies of War
    d. 28-hour day

21. _____ is one of the four Ps of the marketing mix. The other three aspects are product, promotion, and place. It is also a key variable in microeconomic price allocation theory.
    a. Penetration pricing
    b. Price floor
    c. Transfer pricing
    d. Pricing

22. _____ is the management of the flow of goods, information and other resources, including energy and people, between the point of origin and the point of consumption in order to meet the requirements of consumers (frequently, and originally, military organizations.) _____ involves the integration of information, transportation, inventory, warehousing, material-handling, and packaging, and occasionally security. _____ is a channel of the supply chain which adds the value of time and place utility.
    a. 1990 Clean Air Act
    b. Third-party logistics
    c. 28-hour day
    d. Logistics

23. _____ is one of the four elements of marketing mix. An organization or set of organizations (go-betweens) involved in the process of making a product or service available for use or consumption by a consumer or business user.

The other three parts of the marketing mix are product, pricing, and promotion.

    a. Job creation programs
    b. Missing completely at random
    c. Matching theory
    d. Distribution

Chapter 6. Customer Analysis

1. _____ consists of the processes a company uses to track and organize its contacts with its current and prospective customers. _____ software is used to support these processes; information about customers and customer interactions can be entered, stored and accessed by employees in different company departments. Typical _____ goals are to improve services provided to customers, and to use customer contact information for targeted marketing.

    a. Disruptive technology
    b. Marketing plan
    c. Green marketing
    d. Customer relationship management

2. Procter is a surname, and may also refer to:

    - Bryan Waller Procter (pseud. Barry Cornwall), English poet
    - Goodwin Procter, American law firm
    - _____, consumer products multinational

    a. Downstream
    b. Strict liability
    c. Procter ' Gamble
    d. Master and Servant Acts

3. _____ is a concept related to the relative abilities of parties in a situation to exert influence over each other. If both parties are on an equal footing in a debate, then they will have equal _____, such as in a perfectly competitive market, or between an evenly matched monopoly and monopsony.

    There are a number of fields where the concept of _____ has proven crucial to coherent analysis: game theory, labour economics, collective bargaining arrangements, diplomatic negotiations, settlement of litigation, the price of insurance, and any negotiation in general.

    a. Trade credit
    b. Buy-sell agreement
    c. Bargaining power
    d. 1990 Clean Air Act

4. _____ or _____ data refers to selected population characteristics as used in government, marketing or opinion research, or the _____ profiles used in such research. Note the distinction from the term 'demography' Commonly-used _____s include race, age, income, disabilities, mobility (in terms of travel time to work or number of vehicles available), educational attainment, home ownership, employment status, and even location.

Chapter 6. Customer Analysis

   a. Affiliation
   b. Abraham Harold Maslow
   c. Adam Smith
   d. Demographic

5. _____ is a broad label that refers to any individuals or households that use goods and services generated within the economy. The concept of a _____ is used in different contexts, so that the usage and significance of the term may vary.

Typically when business people and economists talk of _____s they are talking about person as _____, an aggregated commodity item with little individuality other than that expressed in the buy/not-buy decision.

   a. 33 Strategies of War
   b. Consumer
   c. 1990 Clean Air Act
   d. 28-hour day

6. _____ is a statistical technique that originated in mathematical psychology. Today it is used in many of the social sciences and applied sciences including marketing, product management, and operations research. It is not to be confused with the theory of conjoint measurement.
   a. Semantic differential
   b. Classical test theory
   c. Counternull
   d. Conjoint analysis

7. _____ or clustering is the assignment of a set of observations into subsets (called clusters) so that observations in the same cluster are similar in some sense. Clustering is a method of unsupervised learning, and a common technique for statistical data analysis used in many fields, including machine learning, data mining, pattern recognition, image analysis and bioinformatics.

Besides the term clustering, there are a number of terms with similar meanings, including automatic classification, numerical taxonomy, botryology and typological analysis.

   a. 1990 Clean Air Act
   b. 28-hour day
   c. Decision tree learning
   d. Cluster analysis

8. In statistics, _____ refers to techniques for the modeling and analysis of numerical data consisting of values of a dependent variable and of one or more independent variables The dependent variable in the regression equation is modeled as a function of the independent variables, corresponding parameters, and an error term. The error term is treated as a random variable and represents unexplained variation in the dependent variable.
   a. Stepwise regression
   b. Least squares
   c. Trend analysis
   d. Regression analysis

Chapter 7. Market Potential and Sales Forecasting

1. _____ is the process of estimation in unknown situations. Prediction is a similar, but more general term. Both can refer to estimation of time series, cross-sectional or longitudinal data.
   a. 28-hour day
   b. 1990 Clean Air Act
   c. Forecasting
   d. 33 Strategies of War

2. An _____ is an organization founded and funded by businesses that operate in a specific industry. An industry trade association participates in public relations activities such as advertising, education, political donations, lobbying and publishing, but its main focus is collaboration between companies, or standardization. Associations may offer other services, such as producing conferences, networking or charitable events or offering classes or educational materials.
   a. AAAI
   b. A4e
   c. A Stake in the Outcome
   d. Industry trade group

3. Marketing research is a form of business research and is generally divided into two categories: consumer _____ and business-to-business (B2B) _____, which was previously known as industrial marketing research. Consumer marketing research studies the buying habits of individual people while business-to-business marketing research investigates the markets for products sold by one business to another.

   Consumer _____ is a form of applied sociology that concentrates on understanding the behaviours, whims and preferences, of consumers in a market-based economy, and aims to understand the effects and comparative success of marketing campaigns.

   a. Questionnaire construction
   b. Questionnaire
   c. Mystery shoppers
   d. Market Research

4. _____ is an integrated communications-based process through which individuals and communities discover that existing and newly-identified needs and wants may be satisfied by the products and services of others.

   _____ is defined by the American _____ Association as the activity, set of institutions, and processes for creating, communicating, delivering, and exchanging offerings that have value for customers, clients, partners, and society at large. The term developed from the original meaning which referred literally to going to market, as in shopping, or going to a market to buy or sell goods or services.

a. Marketing
b. Customer relationship management
c. Market development
d. Disruptive technology

5. _____ is a business magazine published by McGraw-Hill. It was first published in 1929 (as The Business Week) under the direction of Malcolm Muir, who was serving as president of the McGraw-Hill Publishing company at the time. Its primary competitors in the national business magazine category are Fortune and Forbes, which are published bi-weekly.
    a. The Wealth of Nations
    b. Democracy in America
    c. BusinessWeek
    d. Hotel Vikas

6. The _____ is a systematic, interactive forecasting method which relies on a panel of independent experts. The carefully selected experts answer questionnaires in two or more rounds. After each round, a facilitator provides an anonymous summary of the experts' forecasts from the previous round as well as the reasons they provided for their judgments.
    a. Quality function deployment
    b. Hoshin Kanri
    c. Learning organization
    d. Delphi Method

7. In statistics, a _____ rolling mean or running average, is a type of finite impulse response filter used to analyze a set of data points by creating a series of averages of different subsets of the full data set. A _____ is not a single number, but it is a set of numbers, each of which is the average of the corresponding subset of a larger set of data points. A _____ may also use unequal weights for each data value in the subset to emphasize particular values in the subset.
    a. Standard deviation
    b. Time series analysis
    c. Moving average
    d. Homoscedastic

8. In statistics, _____ is a technique that can be applied to time series data, either to produce smoothed data for presentation, or to make forecasts. The time series data themselves are a sequence of observations. The observed phenomenon may be an essentially random process, or it may be an orderly, but noisy, process.

a. A4e
b. A Stake in the Outcome
c. AAAI
d. Exponential smoothing

9. In statistics, _____ refers to techniques for the modeling and analysis of numerical data consisting of values of a dependent variable and of one or more independent variables The dependent variable in the regression equation is modeled as a function of the independent variables, corresponding parameters, and an error term. The error term is treated as a random variable and represents unexplained variation in the dependent variable.
    a. Regression analysis
    b. Trend analysis
    c. Stepwise regression
    d. Least squares

10. In statistics and image processing, to smooth a data set is to create an approximating function that attempts to capture important patterns in the data, while leaving out noise or other fine-scale structures/rapid phenomena. Many different algorithms are used in _____. One of the most common algorithms is the 'moving average', often used to try to capture important trends in repeated statistical surveys.
    a. 1990 Clean Air Act
    b. 28-hour day
    c. 33 Strategies of War
    d. Smoothing

11. In economics, _____s are key economic variables that economists used to predict a new phase of the business cycle. A _____ is one that changes before the economy does; a lagging indicator is one that changes after the economy has changed. Examples of _____s include stock prices, which often improve or worsen before a similar change in the economy.
    a. Perfect competition
    b. Human capital
    c. Deflation
    d. Leading indicator

12. _____s are statistical models used in econometrics. An _____ specifies the statistical relationship that is believed to hold between the various economic quantities pertaining a particular economic phenomena under study. An _____ can be derived from a deterministic economic model by allowing for uncertainty or from an economic model which itself is stochastic.

a. A Stake in the Outcome
b. Econometric model
c. AAAI
d. A4e

13. _____ of the learning curve effect and the closely related experience curve effect express the relationship between equations for experience and efficiency or between efficiency gains and investment in the effort. The experience of 'learning curves' was first observed by the 19th Century German psychologist Hermann Ebbinghaus according to the difficulty of memorizing varying numbers of verbal stimuli, and subsequent learning about the complex processes of learning are discussed in the

.

The rule used for representing the learning curve effect states that the more times a task has been performed, the less time will be required on each subsequent iteration.

a. Spatial Decision Support Systems
b. Point biserial correlation coefficient
c. Models
d. Distribution

Chapter 8. Developing Product Strategy

1. _____ is a business magazine published by McGraw-Hill. It was first published in 1929 (as The Business Week) under the direction of Malcolm Muir, who was serving as president of the McGraw-Hill Publishing company at the time. Its primary competitors in the national business magazine category are Fortune and Forbes, which are published bi-weekly.
    a. BusinessWeek
    b. Hotel Vikas
    c. Democracy in America
    d. The Wealth of Nations

2. A _____ strategy targets non-buying customers in currently targeted segments. It also targets new customers in new segments. (Winer)

A marketing manager has to think about the following questions before implementing a _____ strategy: Is it profitable? Will it require the introduction of new or modified products? Is the customer and channel well enough researched and understood?

The marketing manager uses these four groups to give more focus to the market segment decision: existing customers, competitor customers, non-buying in current segments, new segments.

   a. Context analysis
   b. Customer relationship management
   c. Market development
   d. Product line

3. _____ is one of the four growth strategies of the Product-Market Growth Matrix defined by Ansoff. _____ occurs when a company enters/penetrates a market with current products. The best way to achieve this is by gaining competitors' customers (part of their market share.)
   a. 28-hour day
   b. 33 Strategies of War
   c. 1990 Clean Air Act
   d. Market penetration

4. In marketing, _____ has come to mean the process by which marketers try to create an image or identity in the minds of their target market for its product, brand, or organization. It is the 'relative competitive comparison' their product occupies in a given market as perceived by the target market.

Re-_____ involves changing the identity of a product, relative to the identity of competing products, in the collective minds of the target market.

a. Customer analytics
b. Positioning
c. Context analysis
d. PEST analysis

5. _____ consists of the mental process of thinking involved with the process of judging the merits of multiple options and selecting one of them for action. Some simple examples include deciding whether to get up in the morning or go back to sleep, or selecting a given route for a journey. More complex examples (often decisions that affect what a person thinks or their core beliefs) include choosing a lifestyle, religious affiliation, or political position.

a. Championship mobilization
b. Trade study
c. Groups decision making
d. Choice

6. _____ is a graphics technique used by asset marketers that attempts to visually display the perceptions of customers or potential customers. Typically the position of a product, product line, brand, or company is displayed relative to their competition.

Perceptual maps can have any number of dimensions but the most common is two dimensions.

a. Mass marketing
b. Perceptual mapping
c. Product differentiation
d. PEST analysis

7. Procter is a surname, and may also refer to:

- Bryan Waller Procter (pseud. Barry Cornwall), English poet
- Goodwin Procter, American law firm
- _____, consumer products multinational

a. Procter ' Gamble
b. Strict liability
c. Master and Servant Acts
d. Downstream

Chapter 8. Developing Product Strategy

8. A _____ is a name or trademark connected with a product or producer. _____s have become increasingly important components of culture and the economy, now being described as 'cultural accessories and personal philosophies'.

Some people distinguish the psychological aspect of a _____ from the experiential aspect.

a. Brand loyalty
b. Brand extension
c. Brand
d. Brand awareness

9. _____ is a marketing concept that refers to a consumer knowing of a brand's existence; at aggregate (brand) level it refers to the proportion of consumers who know of the brand.

_____ can be measured by showing a consumer the brand and asking whether or not they knew of it beforehand. However, in common market research practice a variety of recognition and recall measures of _____ are employed all of which test the brand name's association to a product category cue, this came about because most market research in the 20th Century was conducted by post or telephone, actually showing the brand to consumers usually required more expensive face-to-face interviews (until web-based interviews became possible.)

a. Channel conflict
b. Brand loyalty
c. Brand awareness
d. Brand management

10. _____, in marketing, consists of a consumer's commitment to repurchase or otherwise continue using the brand and can be demonstrated by repeated buying of a product or service or other positive behaviors such as word of mouth advocacy.

_____ is more than simple repurchasing, however. Customers may repurchase a brand due to situational constraints, a lack of viable alternatives, or out of convenience.

a. Brand awareness
b. Brand extension
c. Brand image
d. Brand loyalty

Chapter 8. Developing Product Strategy

11. _____ is a broad label that refers to any individuals or households that use goods and services generated within the economy. The concept of a _____ is used in different contexts, so that the usage and significance of the term may vary.

Typically when business people and economists talk of _____s they are talking about person as _____, an aggregated commodity item with little individuality other than that expressed in the buy/not-buy decision.

   a. 1990 Clean Air Act
   b. 28-hour day
   c. Consumer
   d. 33 Strategies of War

12. In business and accounting, _____s are everything of value that is owned by a person or company. Any property or object of value that one possesses, usually considered as applicable to the payment of one's debts is considered an _____. Simplistically stated, _____s are things of value that can be readily converted into cash.
   a. A Stake in the Outcome
   b. AAAI
   c. Asset
   d. A4e

Chapter 9. New Products

1. In probability theory, a probability distribution is called _____ if its cumulative distribution function is _____. This is equivalent to saying that for random variables X with the distribution in question, Pr[X = a] = 0 for all real numbers a, i.e.: the probability that X attains the value a is zero, for any number a. If the distribution of X is _____ then X is called a _____ random variable.
    a. Decision tree pruning
    b. Continuous
    c. Connectionist expert systems
    d. Pay Band

2. A _____ is a name or trademark connected with a product or producer. _____s have become increasingly important components of culture and the economy, now being described as 'cultural accessories and personal philosophies'.

    Some people distinguish the psychological aspect of a _____ from the experiential aspect.

    a. Brand awareness
    b. Brand extension
    c. Brand loyalty
    d. Brand

3. _____ or brand stretching is a marketing strategy in which a firm marketing a product with a well-developed image uses the same brand name in a different product category. Organizations use this strategy to increase and leverage brand equity (definition: the net worth and long-term sustainability just from the renowned name.) An example of a _____ is Jello-gelatin creating Jello pudding pops.
    a. Brand extension
    b. Channel conflict
    c. Brand image
    d. Brand awareness

4. A _____ is a form of qualitative research in which a group of people are asked about their attitude towards a product, service, concept, advertisement, idea, or packaging. Questions are asked in an interactive group setting where participants are free to talk with other group members.

    The first _____s were created at the Bureau of Applied Social Research by associate director, sociologist Robert K. Merton.

a. 1990 Clean Air Act
b. Market analysis
c. Focus group
d. Marketing research

5. Marketing research is a form of business research and is generally divided into two categories: consumer _____ and business-to-business (B2B) _____, which was previously known as industrial marketing research. Consumer marketing research studies the buying habits of individual people while business-to-business marketing research investigates the markets for products sold by one business to another.

Consumer _____ is a form of applied sociology that concentrates on understanding the behaviours, whims and preferences, of consumers in a market-based economy, and aims to understand the effects and comparative success of marketing campaigns.

a. Mystery shoppers
b. Questionnaire
c. Questionnaire construction
d. Market research

6. _____ is the process of estimation in unknown situations. Prediction is a similar, but more general term. Both can refer to estimation of time series, cross-sectional or longitudinal data.
a. 1990 Clean Air Act
b. Forecasting
c. 33 Strategies of War
d. 28-hour day

7. A _____ is a professional who provides advice in a particular area of expertise such as management, accountancy, the environment, entertainment, technology, law, human resources, marketing, medicine, finance, economics, public affairs, communication, engineering, sound system design, graphic design, or waste management.

A _____ is usually an expert or a professional in a specific field and has a wide knowledge of the subject matter. A _____ usually works for a consultancy firm or is self-employed, and engages with multiple and changing clients.

a. 1990 Clean Air Act
b. 28-hour day
c. Consultant
d. 33 Strategies of War

Chapter 10. Pricing Decisions

1. _____ is one of the four Ps of the marketing mix. The other three aspects are product, promotion, and place. It is also a key variable in microeconomic price allocation theory.
    a. Transfer pricing
    b. Price floor
    c. Pricing
    d. Penetration pricing

2. _____ exists when sales of identical goods or services are transacted at different prices from the same provider. In a theoretical market with perfect information, no transaction costs or prohibition on secondary exchange (or re-selling) to prevent arbitrage, _____ can only be a feature of monopoly and oligopoly markets, where market power can be exercised. Otherwise, the moment the seller tries to sell the same good at different prices, the buyer at the lower price can arbitrage by selling to the consumer buying at the higher price but with a tiny discount.
    a. Pricing objectives
    b. Target costing
    c. Price points
    d. Price discrimination

3. _____ is an integrated communications-based process through which individuals and communities discover that existing and newly-identified needs and wants may be satisfied by the products and services of others.

_____ is defined by the American _____ Association as the activity, set of institutions, and processes for creating, communicating, delivering, and exchanging offerings that have value for customers, clients, partners, and society at large. The term developed from the original meaning which referred literally to going to market, as in shopping, or going to a market to buy or sell goods or services.

    a. Market development
    b. Marketing
    c. Customer relationship management
    d. Disruptive technology

4. A _____ is a process that can allow an organization to concentrate its limited resources on the greatest opportunities to increase sales and achieve a sustainable competitive advantage. A _____ should be centered around the key concept that customer satisfaction is the main goal.

A _____ is a written plan which combines product development, promotion, distribution, and pricing approach, identifies the firm's marketing goals, and explains how they will be achieved within a stated timeframe.

a. Disruptive technology
b. Product bundling
c. Category management
d. Marketing strategy

5. _____s are expenses that change in proportion to the activity of a business. In other words, _____ is the sum of marginal costs. It can also be considered normal costs.
   a. Cost accounting
   b. Cost overrun
   c. Variable cost
   d. Fixed costs

6. In economics, business, retail, and accounting, a _____ is the value of money that has been used up to produce something, and hence is not available for use anymore. In economics, a _____ is an alternative that is given up as a result of a decision. In business, the _____ may be one of acquisition, in which case the amount of money expended to acquire it is counted as _____.
   a. Cost
   b. Fixed costs
   c. Cost allocation
   d. Cost overrun

7. _____ is a broad label that refers to any individuals or households that use goods and services generated within the economy. The concept of a _____ is used in different contexts, so that the usage and significance of the term may vary.

Typically when business people and economists talk of _____s they are talking about person as _____, an aggregated commodity item with little individuality other than that expressed in the buy/not-buy decision.

   a. 28-hour day
   b. Consumer
   c. 33 Strategies of War
   d. 1990 Clean Air Act

8. _____ is a worldwide management consulting firm that focuses on solving issues of concern to senior management. McKinsey serves as an advisor to the world's leading businesses, governments, and institutions. It is widely recognized as a leader and one of the most prestigious firms in the management consulting industry.

a. McKinsey ' Company
b. 1990 Clean Air Act
c. 28-hour day
d. 33 Strategies of War

9. _____ is the pricing technique of setting a relatively low initial entry price, often lower than the eventual market price, to attract new customers. The strategy works on the expectation that customers will switch to the new brand because of the lower price. _____ is most commonly associated with a marketing objective of increasing market share or sales volume, rather than to make profit in the short term.
   a. Transfer pricing
   b. Pricing objectives
   c. Price war
   d. Penetration pricing

10. _____ or goals give direction to the whole pricing process. Determining what your objectives are is the first step in pricing. When deciding on _____ you must consider: 1) the overall financial, marketing, and strategic objectives of the company; 2) the objectives of your product or brand; 3) consumer price elasticity and price points; and 4) the resources you have available.
    a. Pricing objectives
    b. Transfer pricing
    c. Premium pricing
    d. Target costing

11. _____ Management is the succession of strategies used by management as a product goes through its _____. The conditions in which a product is sold changes over time and must be managed as it moves through its succession of stages.

The _____ goes through many phases, involves many professional disciplines, and requires many skills, tools and processes.

   a. Strategic Alliance
   b. Golden handshake
   c. Job hunting
   d. Product life cycle

12. _____ is a concept related to the relative abilities of parties in a situation to exert influence over each other. If both parties are on an equal footing in a debate, then they will have equal _____, such as in a perfectly competitive market, or between an evenly matched monopoly and monopsony.

There are a number of fields where the concept of _____ has proven crucial to coherent analysis: game theory, labour economics, collective bargaining arrangements, diplomatic negotiations, settlement of litigation, the price of insurance, and any negotiation in general.

   a. 1990 Clean Air Act
   b. Buy-sell agreement
   c. Trade credit
   d. Bargaining power

13. There are many important decisions about product and service development and marketing. In the process of product development and marketing we should focus on strategic decisions about product attributes, product branding, product packaging, product labeling and product support services. But product strategy also calls for building a _____.
   a. Context analysis
   b. Product bundling
   c. Marketing strategy
   d. Product line

14. _____, or Value optimized pricing is a business strategy. It sets selling prices on the perceived value to the customer, rather than on the actual cost of the product, the market price, competitors prices, or the historical price.

The goal of value-based pricing is to align price with value delivered.

   a. Chief legal officer
   b. Supervisory board
   c. Centralization
   d. Value based pricing

15. Procter is a surname, and may also refer to:

   - Bryan Waller Procter (pseud. Barry Cornwall), English poet
   - Goodwin Procter, American law firm
   - _____, consumer products multinational

a. Strict liability
b. Downstream
c. Master and Servant Acts
d. Procter ' Gamble

16. _____ is a financial mechanism in which a debtor obtains the right to delay payments to a creditor, for a defined period of time, in exchange for a charge or fee. Essentially, the party that owes money in the present purchases the right to delay the payment until some future date. The discount, or charge, is simply the difference between the original amount owed in the present and the amount that has to be paid in the future to settle the debt.
a. Financial modeling
b. Linear model
c. Ruin theory
d. Discounting

Chapter 11. Advertising Decisions

1. _____ is a form of communication that typically attempts to persuade potential customers to purchase or to consume more of a particular brand of product or service. 'While now central to the contemporary global economy and the reproduction of global production networks, it is only quite recently that _____ has been more than a marginal influence on patterns of sales and production. The formation of modern _____ was intimately bound up with the emergence of new forms of monopoly capitalism around the end of the 19th and beginning of the 20th century as one element in corporate strategies to create, organize and where possible control markets, especially for mass produced consumer goods.

   a. A Stake in the Outcome
   b. Advertising
   c. AAAI
   d. A4e

2. _____, according to The American Marketing Association, is 'a planning process designed to assure that all brand contacts received by a customer or prospect for a product, service, or organization are relevant to that person and consistent over time.'

   _____ is a term used to describe a holistic approach to marketing. It aims to ensure consistency of message and the complementary use of media. The concept includes online and offline marketing channels.

   a. A Stake in the Outcome
   b. A4e
   c. AAAI
   d. Integrated marketing communications

3. _____ is an integrated communications-based process through which individuals and communities discover that existing and newly-identified needs and wants may be satisfied by the products and services of others.

   _____ is defined by the American _____ Association as the activity, set of institutions, and processes for creating, communicating, delivering, and exchanging offerings that have value for customers, clients, partners, and society at large. The term developed from the original meaning which referred literally to going to market, as in shopping, or going to a market to buy or sell goods or services.

   a. Customer relationship management
   b. Disruptive technology
   c. Market development
   d. Marketing

4. _____s (or MarCom or Integrated _____s) are messages and related media used to communicate with a market. Those who practice advertising, branding, direct marketing, graphic design, marketing, packaging, promotion, publicity, sponsorship, public relations, sales, sales promotion and online marketing are termed marketing communicators, _____ managers, or more briefly as marcom managers.

Chapter 11. Advertising Decisions

Traditionally, _____ practitioners focus on the creation and execution of printed marketing collateral; however, academic and professional research developed the practice to use strategic elements of branding and marketing in order to ensure consistency of message delivery throughout an organization.

   a. Thomas Dale DeLay
   b. Marketing communication
   c. Adam Smith
   d. Abraham Harold Maslow

5. _____ generally refers to a list of all planned expenses and revenues. It is a plan for saving and spending. A _____ is an important concept in microeconomics, which uses a _____ line to illustrate the trade-offs between two or more goods.
   a. 1990 Clean Air Act
   b. Budget
   c. 33 Strategies of War
   d. 28-hour day

6. _____ constitute a class of computer-based information systems including knowledge-based systems that support decision-making activities.

_____ are a specific class of computerized information systems that supports business and organizational decision-making activities. A properly-designed _____ is an interactive software-based system intended to help decision makers compile useful information from raw data, documents, personal knowledge, and/or business models to identify and solve problems and make decisions.

   a. 1990 Clean Air Act
   b. 28-hour day
   c. Spatial Decision Support Systems
   d. Decision support systems

7. _____ is a broad label that refers to any individuals or households that use goods and services generated within the economy. The concept of a _____ is used in different contexts, so that the usage and significance of the term may vary.

Typically when business people and economists talk of _____s they are talking about person as _____, an aggregated commodity item with little individuality other than that expressed in the buy/not-buy decision.

Chapter 11. Advertising Decisions

a. Consumer
b. 1990 Clean Air Act
c. 28-hour day
d. 33 Strategies of War

8. Marketing research is a form of business research and is generally divided into two categories: consumer _____ and business-to-business (B2B) _____, which was previously known as industrial marketing research. Consumer marketing research studies the buying habits of individual people while business-to-business marketing research investigates the markets for products sold by one business to another.

Consumer _____ is a form of applied sociology that concentrates on understanding the behaviours, whims and preferences, of consumers in a market-based economy, and aims to understand the effects and comparative success of marketing campaigns.

a. Market Research
b. Mystery shoppers
c. Questionnaire construction
d. Questionnaire

9. Consumer market research is a form of applied sociology that concentrates on understanding the behaviours, whims and preferences, of consumers in a market-based economy, and aims to understand the effects and comparative success of marketing campaigns. The field of consumer _____ as a statistical science was pioneered by Arthur Nielsen with the founding of the ACNielsen Company in 1923.

Thus _____ is the systematic and objective identification, collection, analysis, and dissemination of information for the purpose of assisting management in decision making related to the identification and solution of problems and opportunities in marketing.

a. Marketing research process
b. 1990 Clean Air Act
c. Market analysis
d. Marketing Research

10. _____ is a business magazine published by McGraw-Hill. It was first published in 1929 (as The Business Week) under the direction of Malcolm Muir, who was serving as president of the McGraw-Hill Publishing company at the time. Its primary competitors in the national business magazine category are Fortune and Forbes, which are published bi-weekly.

a. The Wealth of Nations
b. Democracy in America
c. Hotel Vikas
d. BusinessWeek

11. The _____ captures an expanded spectrum of values and criteria for measuring organizational success: economic, ecological and social. With the ratification of the United Nations and ICLEI _____ standard for urban and community accounting in early 2007, this became the dominant approach to public sector full cost accounting. Similar UN standards apply to natural capital and human capital measurement to assist in measurements required by _____, e.g. the ecoBudget standard for reporting ecological footprint.

a. 1990 Clean Air Act
b. 28-hour day
c. 33 Strategies of War
d. Triple bottom line

12. _____ of the learning curve effect and the closely related experience curve effect express the relationship between equations for experience and efficiency or between efficiency gains and investment in the effort. The experience of 'learning curves' was first observed by the 19th Century German psychologist Hermann Ebbinghaus according to the difficulty of memorizing varying numbers of verbal stimuli, and subsequent learning about the complex processes of learning are discussed in the

.

The rule used for representing the learning curve effect states that the more times a task has been performed, the less time will be required on each subsequent iteration.

a. Spatial Decision Support Systems
b. Models
c. Point biserial correlation coefficient
d. Distribution

Chapter 12. Promotions

1. Procter is a surname, and may also refer to:

   - Bryan Waller Procter (pseud. Barry Cornwall), English poet
   - Goodwin Procter, American law firm
   - _____, consumer products multinational

   a. Procter ' Gamble
   b. Strict liability
   c. Master and Servant Acts
   d. Downstream

2. _____ is one of the four Ps of the marketing mix. The other three aspects are product, promotion, and place. It is also a key variable in microeconomic price allocation theory.
   a. Price floor
   b. Transfer pricing
   c. Pricing
   d. Penetration pricing

3. _____ is an integrated communications-based process through which individuals and communities discover that existing and newly-identified needs and wants may be satisfied by the products and services of others.

   _____ is defined by the American _____ Association as the activity, set of institutions, and processes for creating, communicating, delivering, and exchanging offerings that have value for customers, clients, partners, and society at large. The term developed from the original meaning which referred literally to going to market, as in shopping, or going to a market to buy or sell goods or services.

   a. Disruptive technology
   b. Market development
   c. Customer relationship management
   d. Marketing

4. _____ is a broad label that refers to any individuals or households that use goods and services generated within the economy. The concept of a _____ is used in different contexts, so that the usage and significance of the term may vary.

   Typically when business people and economists talk of _____s they are talking about person as _____, an aggregated commodity item with little individuality other than that expressed in the buy/not-buy decision.

a. 1990 Clean Air Act
b. Consumer
c. 33 Strategies of War
d. 28-hour day

5. A _____, in the field of business and marketing, is a geographic region or demographic group used to gauge the viability of a product or service in the mass market prior to a wide scale roll-out. The criteria used to judge the acceptability of a _____ region or group include:

1. a population that is demographically similar to the proposed target market; and
2. relative isolation from densely populated media markets so that advertising to the test audience can be efficient and economical.

The _____ ideally aims to duplicate 'everything' - promotion and distribution as well as `product' - on a smaller scale. The technique replicates, typically in one area, what is planned to occur in a national launch; and the results are very carefully monitored, so that they can be extrapolated to projected national results. The `area' may be any one of the following:

- Television area

internet online test

- Test town
- Residential neighborhood
- Test site

A number of decisions have to be taken about any _____:

- Which _____?
- What is to be tested?
- How long a test?
- What are the success criteria?

The simple go or no-go decision, together with the related reduction of risk, is normally the main justification for the expense of _____s. At the same time, however, such _____s can be used to test specific elements of a new product's marketing mix; possibly the version of the product itself, the promotional message and media spend, the distribution channels and the price.

a. 1990 Clean Air Act
b. 28-hour day
c. 33 Strategies of War
d. Test market

Chapter 13. Channel Management

1. A _____ is a commercial building for storage of goods. _____s are used by manufacturers, importers, exporters, wholesalers, transport businesses, customs, etc. They are usually large plain buildings in industrial areas of cities and towns.
   a. 33 Strategies of War
   b. 1990 Clean Air Act
   c. 28-hour day
   d. Warehouse

2. _____ is an advertisement in which a particular product specifically mentions a competitor by name for the express purpose of showing why the competitor is inferior to the product naming it.

   This should not be confused with parody advertisements, where a fictional product is being advertised for the purpose of poking fun at the particular advertisement, nor should it be confused with the use of a coined brand name for the purpose of comparing the product without actually naming an actual competitor. ('Wikipedia tastes better and is less filling than the Encyclopedia Galactica.')

   In the 1980s, during what has been referred to as the cola wars, soft-drink manufacturer Pepsi ran a series of advertisements where people, caught on hidden camera, in a blind taste test, chose Pepsi over rival Coca-Cola.

   a. Comparative advertising
   b. 1990 Clean Air Act
   c. 28-hour day
   d. 33 Strategies of War

3. _____ refers to the difference between the cost of materials purchased by a company plus the cost of the labor to assemble a product and the price at which the company sells the product. An example is the price of gasoline at the pump over the price of the oil in it. In national accounts used in macroeconomics, it refers to the contribution of the factors of production, i.e., land, labor, and capital goods, to raising the value of a product and corresponds to the incomes received by the owners of these factors.
   a. Rehn-Meidner Model
   b. Minimum wage
   c. Deregulation
   d. Value added

4. Wholesaling, jobbing to industrial, commercial, institutional or to other _____ and related subordinated services.

   According to the United Nations Statistics Division, 'wholesale' is the resale (sale without transformation) of new and used goods to retailers, to industrial, commercial, institutional or professional users or involves acting as an agent or broker in buying merchandise for such persons or companies. _____ frequently physically assemble, sort and grade goods in large lots, break bulk, repack and redistribute in smaller lots.

a. Supply chain management
b. Supply chain
c. Packaging
d. Wholesalers

5. A _____ is a relatively new executive level position at a corporation, company, organization typically reporting directly to the CEO or board of directors. The _____ is responsible for a brand's image, experience, and promise, and propagating it throughout all aspects of the company. The brand officer oversees marketing, advertising, design, public relations and customer service departments.
   a. Chief brand officer
   b. Purchasing manager
   c. Chief executive officer
   d. Director of communications

6. In political science and economics, the _____ or agency dilemma treats the difficulties that arise under conditions of incomplete and asymmetric information when a principal hires an agent, such as the problem that the two may not have the same interests, while the principal is, presumably, hiring the agent to pursue the interests of the former.

Various mechanisms may be used to try to align the interests of the agent with those of the principal, such as piece rates/commissions, profit sharing, efficiency wages, performance measurement (including financial statements), the agent posting a bond, or fear of firing. The _____ is found in most employer/employee relationships, for example, when stockholders hire top executives of corporations.

   a. 1990 Clean Air Act
   b. 28-hour day
   c. 33 Strategies of War
   d. Principal-agent problem

7. _____ is a sub-discipline and type of marketing. There are two main definitional characteristics which distinguish it from other types of marketing. The first is that it attempts to send its messages directly to consumers, without the use of intervening media.
   a. 28-hour day
   b. 1990 Clean Air Act
   c. Guthy-Renker
   d. Direct marketing

8. _____ is an integrated communications-based process through which individuals and communities discover that existing and newly-identified needs and wants may be satisfied by the products and services of others.

Chapter 13. Channel Management

_____ is defined by the American _____ Association as the activity, set of institutions, and processes for creating, communicating, delivering, and exchanging offerings that have value for customers, clients, partners, and society at large. The term developed from the original meaning which referred literally to going to market, as in shopping, or going to a market to buy or sell goods or services.

  a. Disruptive technology
  b. Customer relationship management
  c. Market development
  d. Marketing

9. _____ is a method of direct marketing in which a salesperson solicits to prospective customers to buy products or services, either over the phone or through a subsequent face to face or Web conferencing appointment scheduled during the call.

_____ can also include recorded sales pitches programmed to be played over the phone via automatic dialing. _____ has come under fire in recent years, being viewed as an annoyance by many.

  a. 1990 Clean Air Act
  b. Telemarketing
  c. 33 Strategies of War
  d. 28-hour day

10. _____, in microeconomics, are the cost advantages that a business obtains due to expansion. They are factors that cause a producer's average cost per unit to fall as scale is increased. _____ is a long run concept and refers to reductions in unit cost as the size of a facility, or scale, increases.
  a. Economies of scope
  b. A Stake in the Outcome
  c. A4e
  d. Economies of scale

11. The _____ is an independent agency of the United States government, established in 1914 by the _____ Act. Its principal mission is the promotion of 'consumer protection' and the elimination and prevention of what regulators perceive to be harmfully 'anti-competitive' business practices, such as coercive monopoly.

The _____ Act was one of President Wilson's major acts against trusts.

a. 33 Strategies of War
b. Federal Trade Commission
c. 1990 Clean Air Act
d. 28-hour day

Chapter 14. Customer Relationship Management

1. _____ consists of the processes a company uses to track and organize its contacts with its current and prospective customers. _____ software is used to support these processes; information about customers and customer interactions can be entered, stored and accessed by employees in different company departments. Typical _____ goals are to improve services provided to customers, and to use customer contact information for targeted marketing.
    a. Disruptive technology
    b. Customer relationship management
    c. Green marketing
    d. Marketing plan

2. The phrase mergers and _____s refers to the aspect of corporate strategy, corporate finance and management dealing with the buying, selling and combining of different companies that can aid, finance, or help a growing company in a given industry grow rapidly without having to create another business entity.

    An _____, also known as a takeover or a buyout, is the buying of one company (the 'target') by another. An _____ may be friendly or hostile.

    a. AAAI
    b. A4e
    c. A Stake in the Outcome
    d. Acquisition

3. In economics, business, retail, and accounting, a _____ is the value of money that has been used up to produce something, and hence is not available for use anymore. In economics, a _____ is an alternative that is given up as a result of a decision. In business, the _____ may be one of acquisition, in which case the amount of money expended to acquire it is counted as _____.
    a. Fixed costs
    b. Cost overrun
    c. Cost
    d. Cost allocation

4. _____ is the process of extracting hidden patterns from data. As more data is gathered, with the amount of data doubling every three years, _____ is becoming an increasingly important tool to transform this data into information. It is commonly used in a wide range of profiling practices, such as marketing, surveillance, fraud detection and scientific discovery.
    a. Data mining
    b. Decision tree learning
    c. 1990 Clean Air Act
    d. 28-hour day

Chapter 14. Customer Relationship Management

5. _____ is an integrated communications-based process through which individuals and communities discover that existing and newly-identified needs and wants may be satisfied by the products and services of others.

_____ is defined by the American _____ Association as the activity, set of institutions, and processes for creating, communicating, delivering, and exchanging offerings that have value for customers, clients, partners, and society at large. The term developed from the original meaning which referred literally to going to market, as in shopping, or going to a market to buy or sell goods or services.

a. Disruptive technology
b. Customer relationship management
c. Market development
d. Marketing

6. _____ is a form of marketing developed from direct response marketing campaigns conducted in the 1970s and 1980s which emphasizes customer retention and satisfaction, rather than a dominant focus on point-of-sale transactions.

_____ differs from other forms of marketing in that it recognizes the long term value to the firm of keeping customers, as opposed to direct or 'Intrusion' marketing, which focuses upon acquisition of new clients by targeting majority demographics based upon prospective client lists.

_____ refers to a long-term and mutually beneficial arrangement wherein both the buyer and seller focus on value enhancement with the goal of providing a more satisfying exchange.

a. 1990 Clean Air Act
b. Guerrilla marketing
c. 28-hour day
d. Relationship marketing

7. _____ is the provision of service to customers before, during and after a purchase.

According to Turban et al. (2002), '_____ is a series of activities designed to enhance the level of customer satisfaction - that is, the feeling that a product or service has met the customer expectation.'

Its importance varies by product, industry and customer; defective or broken merchandise can be exchanged, often only with a receipt and within a specified time frame.

Chapter 14. Customer Relationship Management

a. Service rate
b. 28-hour day
c. 1990 Clean Air Act
d. Customer service

8. _____ is an advertisement in which a particular product specifically mentions a competitor by name for the express purpose of showing why the competitor is inferior to the product naming it.

This should not be confused with parody advertisements, where a fictional product is being advertised for the purpose of poking fun at the particular advertisement, nor should it be confused with the use of a coined brand name for the purpose of comparing the product without actually naming an actual competitor. ('Wikipedia tastes better and is less filling than the Encyclopedia Galactica.')

In the 1980s, during what has been referred to as the cola wars, soft-drink manufacturer Pepsi ran a series of advertisements where people, caught on hidden camera, in a blind taste test, chose Pepsi over rival Coca-Cola.

a. 1990 Clean Air Act
b. 33 Strategies of War
c. 28-hour day
d. Comparative advertising

9. _____s are structured marketing efforts that reward, and therefore encourage, loyal buying behavior -- behavior which is potentially of benefit to the firm.

In marketing generally and in retailing more specifically, a loyalty card, rewards card, points card, advantage card, or club card is a plastic or paper card, visually similar to a credit card or debit card, that identifies the card holder as a member in a _____. Loyalty cards are a system of the loyalty business model.

a. 33 Strategies of War
b. 28-hour day
c. Loyalty program
d. 1990 Clean Air Act

10. _____, in marketing, manufacturing, call centres and management, is the use of flexible computer-aided manufacturing systems to produce custom output. Those systems combine the low unit costs of mass production processes with the flexibility of individual customization.

'_____' is the new frontier in business competition for both manufacturing and service industries.

a. 28-hour day
b. 1990 Clean Air Act
c. 33 Strategies of War
d. Mass customization

Chapter 15. Financial Analysis for Product Management

1. _____ refers to an assessment of the viability, stability and profitability of a business, sub-business or project.

It is performed by professionals who prepare reports using ratios that make use of information taken from financial statements and other reports. These reports are usually presented to top management as one of their bases in making business decisions.

   a. 33 Strategies of War
   b. 1990 Clean Air Act
   c. 28-hour day
   d. Financial analysis

2. _____ is the planning process used to determine whether a firm's long term investments such as new machinery, replacement machinery, new plants, new products, and research development projects are worth pursuing. It is budget for major capital, or investment, expenditures.

Many formal methods are used in _____, including the techniques such as

   - Net present value
   - Profitability index
   - Internal rate of return
   - Modified Internal Rate of Return
   - Equivalent annuity

These methods use the incremental cash flows from each potential investment, or project. Techniques based on accounting earnings and accounting rules are sometimes used - though economists consider this to be improper - such as the accounting rate of return, and 'return on investment.' Simplified and hybrid methods are used as well, such as payback period and discounted payback period.

   a. Gross profit margin
   b. Gross profit
   c. Restricted stock
   d. Capital budgeting

3. _____ is a company's financial statement that indicates how the revenue is transformed into the net income The purpose of the _____ is to show managers and investors whether the company made or lost money during the period being reported.

The important thing to remember about an _____ is that it represents a period of time.

Chapter 15. Financial Analysis for Product Management

a. A4e
b. A Stake in the Outcome
c. AAAI
d. Income statement

4. In cost-volume-profit analysis, a form of management accounting, _____ is the marginal profit per unit sale. It is a useful quantity in carrying out various calculations, and can be used as a measure of operating leverage.

The Total _____ is Total Revenue (TR, or Sales) minus Total Variable Cost (TVC):

TContribution margin = TR − TVC

The Unit _____ (C) is Unit Revenue (Price, P) minus Unit Variable Cost (V):

C = P − V

The _____ Ratio is the percentage of Contribution over Total Revenue, which can be calculated from the unit contribution over unit price or total contribution over Total Revenue:

$$\frac{C}{P} = \frac{P-V}{P} = \frac{\text{Unit Contribution Margin}}{\text{Price}} = \frac{\text{Total Contribution Margin}}{\text{Total Revenue}}$$

For instance, if the price is $10 and the unit variable cost is $2, then the unit _____ is $8, and the _____ ratio is $8/$10 = 80%.

a. Customer profitability
b. Factory overhead
c. Profit center
d. Contribution margin

5. In economics, business, retail, and accounting, a _____ is the value of money that has been used up to produce something, and hence is not available for use anymore. In economics, a _____ is an alternative that is given up as a result of a decision. In business, the _____ may be one of acquisition, in which case the amount of money expended to acquire it is counted as _____.

a. Cost overrun
b. Fixed costs
c. Cost allocation
d. Cost

Chapter 15. Financial Analysis for Product Management

6. Models of the learning curve effect and the closely related _____ effect express the relationship between equations for experience and efficiency or between efficiency gains and investment in the effort. The experience of 'learning curves' was first observed by the 19th Century German psychologist Hermann Ebbinghaus according to the difficulty of memorizing varying numbers of verbal stimuli, and subsequent learning about the complex processes of learning are discussed in the

.

The rule used for representing the learning curve effect states that the more times a task has been performed, the less time will be required on each subsequent iteration.

   a. AAAI
   b. A4e
   c. A Stake in the Outcome
   d. Experience curve

7. In economics, _____ are business expenses that are not dependent on the activities of the business They tend to be time-related, such as salaries or rents being paid per month. This is in contrast to variable costs, which are volume-related (and are paid per quantity.)

In management accounting, _____ are defined as expenses that do not change in proportion to the activity of a business, within the relevant period or scale of production.

   a. Fixed costs
   b. Cost of quality
   c. Cost allocation
   d. Transaction cost

8. _____s are expenses that change in proportion to the activity of a business. In other words, _____ is the sum of marginal costs. It can also be considered normal costs.
   a. Cost overrun
   b. Variable cost
   c. Cost accounting
   d. Fixed costs

9. _____ is one of the managerial functions like planning, organizing, staffing and directing. It is an important function because it helps to check the errors and to take the corrective action so that deviation from standards are minimized and stated goals of the organization are achieved in desired manner.According to modern concepts, _____ is a foreseeing action whereas earlier concept of _____ was used only when errors were detected. _____ in management means setting standards, measuring actual performance and taking corrective action.

Chapter 15. Financial Analysis for Product Management

a. Decision tree pruning
b. Schedule of reinforcement
c. Turnover
d. Control

10. The _____ is a rate of return used in capital budgeting to measure and compare the profitability of investments. It is also called the discounted cash flow rate of return (DCFROR) or simply the rate of return (ROR.) In the context of savings and loans the IRR is also called the effective interest rate.

a. AAAI
b. A Stake in the Outcome
c. Internal Rate of Return
d. A4e

11. In finance, _____, is the ratio of money gained or lost on an investment relative to the amount of money invested. The amount of money gained or lost may be referred to as interest, profit/loss, gain/loss, or net income/loss. The money invested may be referred to as the asset, capital, principal, or the cost basis of the investment.

a. Return on sales
b. Return on Capital Employed
c. Financial ratio
d. Rate of Return

12. In corporate finance, _____ or _____ is an estimate of true economic profit after making corrective adjustments to GAAP accounting, including deducting the opportunity cost of equity capital. _____ can be measured as Net Operating Profit After Taxes(or NOPAT) less the money cost of capital. _____ is similar in nature to that of calculating another financial performance measure - Residual Income , however, there are a few complexities involved with coming up with the elements for calculating _____ over RI such as the myriad adjustments that might be made to NOPAT before it is suitable for the formula below.

a. A4e
b. A Stake in the Outcome
c. AAAI
d. Economic value added

13. _____ is the value on a given date of a future payment or series of future payments, discounted to reflect the time value of money and other factors such as investment risk. _____ calculations are widely used in business and economics to provide a means to compare cash flows at different times on a meaningful 'like to like' basis.

If offered a choice between $100 today or $100 in one year, everyone will choose $100 today.

Chapter 15. Financial Analysis for Product Management

a. Present value
b. 1990 Clean Air Act
c. Net present value
d. Discounted cash flow

14. _____ refers to the difference between the cost of materials purchased by a company plus the cost of the labor to assemble a product and the price at which the company sells the product. An example is the price of gasoline at the pump over the price of the oil in it. In national accounts used in macroeconomics, it refers to the contribution of the factors of production, i.e., land, labor, and capital goods, to raising the value of a product and corresponds to the incomes received by the owners of these factors.
    a. Rehn-Meidner Model
    b. Value added
    c. Deregulation
    d. Minimum wage

Chapter 16. Marketing Metrics

1. _____ is an integrated communications-based process through which individuals and communities discover that existing and newly-identified needs and wants may be satisfied by the products and services of others.

_____ is defined by the American _____ Association as the activity, set of institutions, and processes for creating, communicating, delivering, and exchanging offerings that have value for customers, clients, partners, and society at large. The term developed from the original meaning which referred literally to going to market, as in shopping, or going to a market to buy or sell goods or services.

   a. Market development
   b. Disruptive technology
   c. Marketing
   d. Customer relationship management

2. The _____ is a concept from business management that was first described and popularized by Michael Porter in his 1985 best-seller, Competitive Advantage: Creating and Sustaining Superior Performance.

A _____ is a chain of activities. Products pass through all activities of the chain in order and at each activity the product gains some value. The chain of activities gives the products more added value than the sum of added values of all activities. It is important not to mix the concept of the _____ with the costs occurring throughout the activities.

   a. Market development
   b. Customer relationship management
   c. Mass marketing
   d. Value chain

3. In business and accounting, _____s are everything of value that is owned by a person or company. Any property or object of value that one possesses, usually considered as applicable to the payment of one's debts is considered an _____. Simplistically stated, _____s are things of value that can be readily converted into cash.
   a. AAAI
   b. A4e
   c. A Stake in the Outcome
   d. Asset

4. A _____ is a name or trademark connected with a product or producer. _____s have become increasingly important components of culture and the economy, now being described as 'cultural accessories and personal philosophies'.

Some people distinguish the psychological aspect of a _____ from the experiential aspect.

a. Brand extension
b. Brand awareness
c. Brand loyalty
d. Brand

5. The _____ is generally accepted as the use and specification of the 'four P's' describing the strategic position of a product in the marketplace. One version of the _____ originated in 1948 when James Culliton said that a marketing decision should be a result of something similar to a recipe. This version was used in 1953 when Neil Borden, in his American Marketing Association presidential address, took the recipe idea one step further and coined the term 'marketing-mix'.
   a. Marketing mix
   b. 1990 Clean Air Act
   c. 33 Strategies of War
   d. 28-hour day

ANSWER KEY

Chapter 1
1. a 2. c 3. b 4. a 5. d

Chapter 2
1. d 2. a 3. a 4. c 5. d 6. d 7. d

Chapter 3
1. a 2. d 3. b 4. d

Chapter 4
1. d 2. d 3. d 4. a 5. d 6. d 7. a 8. c 9. b 10. d
11. b 12. c

Chapter 5
1. d 2. d 3. b 4. d 5. d 6. c 7. a 8. c 9. d 10. d
11. a 12. d 13. d 14. d 15. a 16. d 17. d 18. d 19. d 20. a
21. d 22. d 23. d

Chapter 6
1. d 2. c 3. c 4. d 5. b 6. d 7. d 8. d

Chapter 7
1. c 2. d 3. d 4. a 5. c 6. d 7. c 8. d 9. a 10. d
11. d 12. b 13. c

Chapter 8
1. a 2. c 3. d 4. b 5. d 6. b 7. a 8. c 9. c 10. d
11. c 12. c

Chapter 9
1. b 2. d 3. a 4. c 5. d 6. b 7. c

Chapter 10
1. c 2. d 3. b 4. d 5. c 6. a 7. b 8. a 9. d 10. a
11. d 12. d 13. d 14. d 15. d 16. d

Chapter 11
1. b 2. d 3. d 4. b 5. b 6. d 7. a 8. a 9. d 10. d
11. d 12. b

Chapter 12
1. a 2. c 3. d 4. b 5. d

ANSWER KEY

Chapter 13
1. d   2. a   3. d   4. d   5. a   6. d   7. d   8. d   9. b   10. d
11. b

Chapter 14
1. b   2. d   3. c   4. a   5. d   6. d   7. d   8. d   9. c   10. d

Chapter 15
1. d   2. d   3. d   4. d   5. d   6. d   7. a   8. b   9. d   10. c
11. d   12. d   13. a   14. b

Chapter 16
1. c   2. d   3. d   4. d   5. a

www.ingramcontent.com/pod-product-compliance
Lightning Source LLC
Chambersburg PA
CBHW080743250426
43671CB00038B/2850